A Grateful Path

Other Titles by Marci
Published by
Blue Mountain Arts®

Friends Forever
A Celebration of Friendship and Everything Friends Share
Through the Years

To My Mother
Your Love Is a Lasting Treasure

A Sister Always… A Friend Forever
A Celebration of the Love, Support, and Friendship Sisters Share

Library of Congress Control Number: 2007923651
ISBN: 978-1-59842-249-8

Printed in China.
First printing: 2007

⊕ This book is printed on recycled paper.

This book is printed on fine quality, laid embossed, 80 lb. paper. This paper has been specially produced to be acid free (neutral pH) and contains no groundwood or unbleached pulp. It conforms with all the requirements of the American National Standards Institute, Inc., so as to ensure that this book will last and be enjoyed by future generations.

Blue Mountain Arts, Inc.
P.O. Box 4549, Boulder, Colorado 80306

A Grateful Path

Inspirational Thoughts on
Unconditional Love, Acceptance,
and Positive Living

Marci

Blue Mountain Press™
Boulder, Colorado

Introduction

I believe life is a journey home. Home is that place I call "acceptance." A great sense of peace comes with acknowledgment, understanding, and belief that each person who has come into our lives has been just the right person we needed for growth at that time.

As we realize that we have a choice about the way we see our relationships and we accept the challenge to see each in a positive light and learn, we can experience a deep sense of gratitude — one of life's greatest gifts.

It is with great joy and gratitude that I'm sharing this book with you.

Marci

Choose Your Path

Your life holds for you endless possibilities.
Do what is necessary to move forward one
day at a time. Keep sight always of what
is important in life. Remember that true
happiness and purpose will be found in
relationships — in the workplace and at
home. Live each day open to guidance,
and your purpose will be revealed to you.

Discover Your Unique Talents

Cultivate your unique talents; let your "inner light" shine. Recognize your talents and strengths, remembering that they are both a gift and a responsibility.

Listen when people tell you that you are good at something — they are seeing your "inner light!"

Get out all your favorite books,
and put them in a pile. There
are clues there to who you are,
what your unique talents are.

When you know who you are,
you have a frame of reference
for every decision you make.

Integrity is priceless — don't
exchange it for money or fame.

Acceptance Is the Key

One of life's paradoxes:
Accept yourself — you change.
Accept others — they change.

Allow others in your life the time
they need to process change and grow.

Remember we cannot really
know what is best for another.

"I don't believe it."
"This isn't happening."
"It's your fault."
"If I do this or that,
could it change things?"
"I don't think I can go on."
If you hear yourself saying any
of these things — you are in the
process of acceptance.

Fighting against the way things are causes
most personal suffering —
acceptance is the path to serenity.

Change Is Good

If life were easy there would be no need
for change — change calls forth
our wisdom and our courage.

One thing in life is certain —
nothing stays the same —
change is inevitable.

If your actions do not match your highest
intentions, it's time for change.

Willingness is the key
to open the door to change.

If you have a negative
attitude — when you
open the door, that is
what you'll find.

Why do some survive the most
horrible of tragedies and maintain
a positive outlook on life?
They have a willing spirit.

Acceptance creates the fertile
soil for change.

Celebrate People's Differences

Give thanks for the
differences in people, and
recognize the opportunity
to see the world from
another view.

Sometimes wisdom comes from
the most unexpected source —
let go of judgments.

Show respect for everyone's
contribution. Without all
the pieces, the puzzle won't
be complete.

Each one of us is a unique individual.
Even if you could stand in another
person's shoes and experience
all he or she has in a lifetime, your
perceptions could be totally different.

Focusing on differences is divisive —
look for common ground.

Have respect for another's beliefs —
it's who they are. Live your own.

Make Sure Your Beliefs
Match Your Actions

If your beliefs and actions
do not match, a thorough
examination of your belief system
may be necessary. Ask: have you
consciously accepted the beliefs
handed down to you as your own?
Make whatever adjustments are necessary
to experience integrity.

You are responsible and accountable for what you believe.

You can either waste a lot of energy convincing others of your position or you can use that energy to move forward and live your beliefs. The second option is very powerful.

To develop one's beliefs and live by them is to know integrity.

Shift Your Attitude

If what you're doing isn't working — do something else.

Always ask: Does it have to be either/or? Can it be both/and?

Just as an athlete trains his body to perform, one can train the mind toward healthy thinking.

It's not the hand you're dealt that counts... but how you play it.

Do the best you can with what you know today and always be willing to learn.

Overcome Fear

If your reactions are based
on fear, the results will not be
a reflection of love — love and
fear are contradictions.

Courage is not the absence of
fear, it is moving forward in
spite of it.

Patience Is a Virtue

Patience is a gift that creates an environment
of safety and promotes spiritual growth.

With the exercise of patience one also calls
in other virtues — love, faith, hope.

Sometimes, when you think
the answer is "no," it is "not yet."

Seek the Positive in All Things, and You Shall Find It

Most of the things in life we have no control over — but we do have a choice about how we see them.

Why do some people see things in a positive light and others in a negative? It's habit. Habits can be changed or developed with focused attention.

Learn to catch yourself when
you start to think negatively —
say to yourself, "Don't go there."

Developing a positive mental attitude takes:
1. Making a decision.
2. Becoming willing to do the work.
3. Action.

Focus on Today

Life is a process, not an event.
All that you experience is necessary
for your understanding.

There are two days in the
week that are not important —
yesterday and tomorrow.
Focus on today.

Looking in the rearview
mirror is fine if you glance
to see what's behind you — but
if you stare too long, you
may crash.

Let go of the past.
Take responsibility for the facts
of your life...
Move forward.

Give Thanks

One of the most useful
lessons we learn in life is one
of the first — always say
please and thank you.

Truly appreciate all
that you have been given,
as well as the things
that you have lost.

Remember always that the
most important things — health,
happiness, and relationships —
come without a price.

Live One Day at a Time

When you have an overwhelming task
at hand, make a decision to do *something*
each day, no matter how small,
and you will be amazed at what
gets accomplished!

Just begin.

Sometimes the road of life takes us to a place we had planned... sometimes it shows us a surprise around the bend we never could have anticipated. We make decisions based on the information we have... We accept the ups and downs as they come... We live "one day at a time." But often we find it is only when we look back that we can see that what we had thought was a "wrong turn" has brought us to exactly the right place and every step was a right one after all!

Make the Most
of Life's Difficult Times

Life can seem so unfair at times, and
we cannot understand the reason for this.
Remember… this too shall pass.

Roadblocks are obstacles that push us
back on track. Focusing inward on our
own choices, instead of trying to move
mountains, frees up energy that turns
roadblocks into steppingstones.

Spending time wishing things were
different is a waste of precious energy.
That energy is better spent on other things.

Everything is relative — could you ever
recognize joy without sorrow?

When a storm bends a tree
to the ground, the roots
become stronger.

Live Without Regret

If you have learned something from every
experience, there should be no regrets.
If you understand that learning is a process,
there are no wrong decisions.

When facing a loss, you can
become bitter or better.
It's your choice.

People make mistakes —
it is part of the human
condition and a very
important part of life. It's
the foundation for empathy
toward our fellow man.

Wisdom comes with experience;
it's usually the painful events
that hold the greatest lessons.

Turn around and look at your
life — you will see that
everything that has happened
to you has put you where
you are today.

Learn to Let Go

One of the most difficult things
to do in life is to "let go."

Fighting the way life is
is like trying to stop a storm…
Put down the umbrella, and
let the rain in.

Life is that dance we do in
the space between
"making it happen" and
"letting it happen."

Think about the big
picture; let go of the
details. Intention is powerful.

Steps to Take

If it has always been done the same way,
maybe it's time to try something new.

To be successful at life, learn how to solve
problems... they always present themselves.

If your day is going
badly, find someone to give
a word of encouragement to.

Go easy on yourself — you'll find then you'll go easy on others.

How do you measure success?
Ask: how happy are you?

How to keep focused on
healthy, positive thinking?
Practice, practice, practice.

You Are Never Alone

Sometimes you may feel that you
are all alone, as life brings
challenges to overcome and
hardships to bear. But when you
least expect it, help will appear…

It may be a kind word from a
stranger or a phone call at
just the right time, and you are
suddenly surrounded with the
loving grace of God.

We don't always
get what we
want... but we
always get
what we need.

Help is always there
when you are ready.

Four Things That Last... Faith, Hope, Friendship, and Love

If you have these things, whatever
challenges life brings, you will get through.
Your faith will light your path... hope
will keep you strong... your friendships
will remind you of what is important
in life... and the love you give
to others will bring you joy.

Explore your faith — live
by it — know happiness.

Everything always works out
as it should, though often it's
just not what you had planned.

Live with faith, and your path in
life will become clear.

After a big storm —
look for a rainbow.

Remember... when fire burns a forest to the ground, everything gets a fresh start.

Friendship

Through the gift of friendship, we are given the opportunity to give and receive love while traveling the journey of life. We can share our hopes and dreams and learn about "our best selves" as we meet the challenges to listen, to give support, and to be there when we are needed. Through the gift of friendship, we are reminded that some things do last forever, and friendship is one of them.

Cherish your friends — remember your lives were brought together for a reason.

Love is not a feeling — love
is an action... love is a choice.

Accept the love of others
as they can give it — this is
the way to experience
unconditional love.

If you are tempted to let people know they have not loved you as you have "wished," remember this is not a demonstration of unconditional love. If you cannot love unconditionally, how can you expect others to? To experience unconditional love, you must not put conditions on it.

When you're tempted to say one more thing — let it be "I love you."

Love is the greatest gift of all!

Learn from Every Relationship

Some of the happiest moments in life
take place in the context
of relationships.

Relationships provide the most
significant opportunity for
spiritual growth — we are
called to be more than we
thought we could be.

If variety is the "spice of life," why do we try to make others see things our way?

Just the right people are present in our lives that we need to grow, so don't try to change them — look within.

Remember that each person has a journey that is not for your understanding.

Forgive

Anger is a very powerful emotion that signals the need for change. Sometimes what is needed is a change in attitude.

Make peace with all those you have loved — even if they have hurt you. If they had been able to do better, they probably would have.

You can't always wait for
feelings to be resolved before
you move on. The moving on is
part of the resolution.

Always acknowledge intention.

Forgiveness is not forgetting…
it is letting go of pain
and letting go of judgment.

Make a Difference

Everyone can make a
difference in the world.
Start at home.

If you want to really be
successful, don't try to
compete — try to contribute.

No matter if you are painting a canvas or a house, sculpting a statue or cutting the grass, singing on a stage or planting flowers in the garden — you are changing the world.

Strive for progress, not perfection.

Follow Your Dreams

As we take our journey through life, we often wonder what will bring us fulfillment. We have a vague sense that we may have a calling, yet we do not know which way to go.

Write down your dream and tuck it away — entrusting that all things will come at the right time.

If you have a dream — go for it. You can never completely eliminate the risks. Don't quit just because it gets hard.

When you are facing a decision and you can't make up your mind, try on each solution in your mind and see how it feels.

Take Some Time...

If you are stuck in thinking
and can't find a solution,
switch gears to physical
activity. Sometimes the
answer will just pop
into your head.

Take some time for quiet reading
and reflection in the morning — your
mind is very open then.

If you're trying to figure out something,
don't force the solution.
Clean out a closet or a drawer
instead — live a metaphor.

When growing up, we often hear the words, "Don't just sit there — do something!" Often the exact opposite is called for.

Confusion can be a gift. It keeps us from moving forward until we have clarity. There's a right time for everything.

Listen and Be Heard

If you have an opportunity to listen — take it. You might be amazed at what you'll hear.

As one listens to another
with loving intent,
the solutions to one's own
problems may be heard.

Silent listening is one of the greatest acts of unconditional love. It's what God does.

When you are very sad, have a good cry. Then find a good listener — someone who will respect your ability to find your own solution.

Set a Good Example

Be a model — sometimes
that's all you can do.

By your
actions you will lift up
the spirit of another.

Kindness is always
in season!

You can best help
others by living
your own life
with integrity.

Let your light shine — brighten
someone's day.

Express Gratitude

Gratitude is a gift you can choose each day.

If you have been gifted with the knowledge
of your unique contribution to the world —
give thanks. If you have a willingness
to know — you will.

Focus only on the positive qualities of those
you love — express gratitude.

Give thanks for each day in advance.

To take credit for everything
that has gone right in our lives
is an attitude that deprives us
of the experience of gratitude.
You also take on the burden
for everything that has not
turned out as you planned.

Express gratitude each day for
what you have, who you are,
and who you have been.

Ten Simple Things
to Remember

1. Love is why we are here.

2. The most important day is today.

3. If you always do your best,
   you will not have regrets.

4. In spite of your best efforts, some things are out of your control.

5. Things always look better tomorrow.

6. Often a wrong turn will bring you to exactly the right place.

7. Sometimes a good laugh is all you need.

8. True friends share your joys, see the best in you, and support you through challenges.

9. If you want to know who you are, ask yourself; listen carefully for the answer.

10. For all your accomplishments, nothing will bring you more happiness than the love you find.

Share Your Special Gifts
with the World

If you have a sincere desire
to share your gifts and your
talents with others, you will be
shown the way.

When you are able to feel the effects of
your actions on others, you have learned
one of life's most important lessons.

If your intention is to share,
you will always have enough.

Success Is Empty Without People You Love to Share It With

When you share joy, it multiplies.
When you share pain, it divides.

Hug the people you love...
and thank them for who they are.

Be the parent you always wanted —
you'll be amazed at how hard it is.

Tell your children they
are valuable — they'll fall in
love with someone who will tell
them the same thing.

The Bonds We Form Are as Everlasting as the Spirit!

Understand and accept that life's greatest purpose can be found in relationships.

It is our connections with our parents, our children, our spouses, our siblings, and our friends that provide us with lasting joy.

Love has no end.

It is often through sharing your gifts and talents with others that your path in life will become clear. It is when you are "giving" that others can see in you that which is known as your "best self."

Life is a journey home.
Home is acceptance.

About Marci

Marci began her career by hand-painting floral designs on clothing. No one was more surprised than she was when one day, in a single burst of inspiration and a completely new and different art style, her delightful characters sprang from her pen! "Their wild and crazy hair is a sign of strength," she thought, "and their crooked little smiles are endearing." She quickly identified the charming characters as Mother, Daughter, Sister, Father, Son, Friend, and so on, until all the people and places in life were filled. Then, with her own loved ones in mind, she wrote a true and special sentiment to each one. This would be the beginning of a wonderful success story, which today still finds Marci writing each and every one of her verses in this same personal way.

Marci is a self-taught artist who has always enjoyed writing and art. She grew up working in her family's small grocery and sub shop. It was there, as she watched her dad interact with customers, she learned that relationships in the workplace and community, as well as in the family, provide the greatest satisfaction and joy.

She went on to develop a business from her home, making home-baked breads, cakes, and pastries to be sold in her dad's store. Later, she started another small home-based business hand-painting clothing for women. At first, she didn't have any idea she could paint and was amazed at how many people loved her work! She was gratified that she could create "wearables" that brought so much joy to those who wore them.

Now as she looks back, Marci sees how all her interests were pieces of a puzzle that fit together and gave her the skills she needed for her work today as artist and author. She is thrilled to see how her delightful characters and universal messages of love have touched the hearts and lives of people everywhere.

FAITH
HOPE
LOVE

All Paths Lead
to Home